FOUNDATIONS

12 LESSONS TO GROW YOUR FAITH

Part 1: Lessons 1–6

CR✝SSWAY
BAPTIST CHURCH

Contents

Preface

It is our prayer that this study will help you to develop a thoughtful, biblical, and consistent walk with the Lord that is based on the biblical revelation of who God is and what he desires for you. Not every lesson will contain new material for everyone. Some people will find certain lessons basic yet beneficial as they assemble the foundational puzzle pieces of Christianity in a logical and coherent way. Please commit to spending time in prayer and the Bible throughout this learning process. Take the time to look up each reference in the text and read the verses carefully. You will greatly benefit from the fellowship and discipline that this study demands.

This program is designed to be an inductive study where you are able to sort through the Bible and answer the study questions on your own. Each lesson concludes with comprehension questions that are designed to help you review and evaluate your understanding of the topic as a whole. The first few lessons are personal and deal with your faith; the lessons that follow will help you understand the basics for growth and Christian service to and with others. Finally, this book cannot replace a local church family that will encourage and teach you to practice these truths. It is our prayer that this series will grow you in God's grace and bring you to a more Christ-like walk, thereby bringing our Savior greater glory.

This edition of *Foundations* was produced for Crossway Baptist Church in Bakersfield, CA. It has been written with significant contribution from Grace Church of Mentor, Ohio.

SALVATION

▶ Introduction

Do you know that the Bible has a lot to say about you? It does! Although it doesn't mention you by name, it does have something to say about every member of the human race, including you. It contains some good news, some bad news, and some great news. Let's start with the good.

▶ You and God

Scripture records Jesus saying, "You search the Scriptures because you think that in them you have eternal life; and it is they that bear witness about me" (John 5:39).

Scripture is unlike any other book. It is not primarily a history book or a rulebook. It is far more than a "roadmap" for life. Scripture is first and foremost God's self-revelation. God explains to us who he is and what he does. It is God's autobiography—his communication to mankind about himself. Therefore, it is appropriate to begin this series of Bible studies with several foundational truths about God:

- God is eternal, without start or end. He is timeless (Psalm 90:2).

- God is absolutely holy. He is set apart from everything that exists; there is no one like him (Isaiah 6:3).

- God is completely sinless and will not allow sin in his presence (Habakkuk 1:13).

- God is infinite in power (Genesis 18:14).

- God is good. He is loving and kind in every action and thought (Psalm 86:5).

- God is absolutely just. Everything he does is morally right and excellent (Psalm 145:17).

- God is love (1 John 4:8).

Scripture assumes God's existence and reveals him to be the Creator of everything that exists. Acknowledging that God is the Creator of everything is the foundation to everything else in the Bible. Read

Genesis 1:1, the first verse of the Bible, and explain it in your own words.

_____

_____

_____

_____

According to Genesis 1:27, where did you come from (what was the pattern)?

_____

_____

Although it is commonly taught that mankind is the result of years and years of evolution apart from any act of God, Scripture teaches clearly and repeatedly that "all things were made through him [Christ]; and without him was not any thing made that was made" (John 1:3). All things were created in six 24-hour days out of nothing (Exodus 20:11)!

Psalm 19:1 tells us that the world around us is like a book that "declares the glory of God." Romans 1:20 adds that creation teaches two key lessons about God: (1) that he exists and (2) that he is powerful. It concludes by saying that those who reject God and his creative power are "without excuse."

The account of man's creation by the creative power of God was not written so that we can answer the modern debate about human origin. It is not merely written for science. Instead, it is written to help us to understand that God's creation of humanity results in two important realities:

1. *Because God made you, you are accountable to him.*

   If you were produced by "chance" as evolution teaches, you would be your own master. You would be answerable to no one. But because you are a creature, you must give an account of your life to your creator. The Bible records a time of future judgment in Revelation 20:11–15 and refers to it as the great white throne. According to verse 12, both "great and small" will appear before God to be judged. Who then must give an answer to God for how they have lived?

   _____

   _____

   What does Hebrews 9:27 say to reinforce this fact?

   _____

   _____

   _____

   ## Principle

   Because God created you, you will be evaluated by Christ, the judge. You will be rewarded or condemned for your life.

2. *Because God made you, he owns you.*

   Like John 1, Colossians 1:16 again teaches, "by him [Christ] all things were created, in Heaven and earth." It concludes by saying, "all things were created _____ him and _____ him."

"The Chief End of Man..."

The Westminster Catechism—a statement of Bible doctrine that has helped to instruct believers since the 17th century—asks students the purpose of God in creation, "What is the chief end of man?" The students are supposed to respond with this statement, "Man's chief end is to glorify God, and to enjoy him forever." Not only did God make you, but he also made you to enjoy him. Enjoyment of God brings you pleasure, and it brings God glory!

Read Revelation 4:11, a record of Christ's worship in heaven. Why is Jesus Christ, who is God, worthy to receive worship— "glory and honor and power"?

_____

_____

_____

Why did God create you? See Isaiah 43:7.

_____

_____

_____

God desires to have fellowship with his people. Read the Bible's account of creation in Genesis 1–3. As far back as the Garden of Eden, God enjoyed walking and talking with his people (Genesis 3:8). Just as God was with Adam and Eve in the garden, he wants to have a relationship with humanity. He wants to enjoy fellowship with people in heaven forever in a sinless and mutually joyful relationship. That's the good news. Sadly, Adam and Eve destroyed their fellowship with God when they sinned (Genesis 3:6). Because of their sin, all people are born sinners with a sinful nature (Romans 5:12; Psalm 51:5). That's the bad news.

Principle

God loves the world. He created humans to glorify him and enjoy him in right fellowship with him forever.

▶ You and Sin

You are not only a sinner from birth (your nature), but you are also a sinner by your own choices (your actions). Explain Romans 3:10–11 in your own words.

_____

_____

_____

_____

Now read Romans 3:23. How many people have sinned?

_____

_____

First John 3:4 says sin is breaking God's law. Where would you find God's law?

_____

_____

Give four examples of sin.

1. _____

2. _____

3. _____

4. _____

God's law is anchored in God's own character. His desire is that his people would reflect him (2 Corinthians 3:18). This makes sin a lack of conforming to God's character (see 1 Peter 1:16).

It is popular today to say that man is "basically good." Yet, Scripture teaches that every man, woman and child is a sinner. Jeremiah 17:9 describes the condition of your heart as "_____ above _____ _____" (ESV).

Principle

You are a sinner, both by birth (nature) and by choice (action).

Isaiah 53:6 summarizes the sinfulness of all men as intentional and determined rebellion against God. Like sheep, we have each "gone astray" from God and chosen our "own way" rather than God's way. The fact that you've sinned is bad news, but it gets worse. Read the following verses and explain what they teach about the effects of sin:

How does sin affect our relationship with God? See Isaiah 59:2.

_____

_____

_____

How does sin affect our qualification for entering into heaven? See Revelation 21:27.

_____

_____

_____

Romans 6:23 makes an important point regarding you and your sin. It says, "The wages of sin is death." What is a wage?

_____

_____

_____

According to Romans 6:23, because you sin, what do you deserve?

_____

_____

Principle

Sin separates you from God and you justly deserve death in God's lake of fire.

The Bible speaks of two deaths. The first is physical death. God promised Adam and Eve that if they sinned, they would "surely die," and they did (Genesis 2:17, 5:5). This is the sense in which we usually think of death.

The second death is far worse than the first death. It is spiritual, eternal death. How does the Bible describe the second death in Revelation 20:10, 14–15 and 21:8 (See also 2 Thessalonians 1:9)?

_____

_____

_____

The truth of eternal damnation is hard for most people to accept, but the Bible teaches that everyone who has sinned deserves to be punished for that sin forever in the lake of fire. Many people think that hell and the lake of fire are just for men like Hitler or Osama bin Laden. But the Bible says that hell is not just for murderers; it is for all sinners! That is not just bad news—it is horrific news!

Too Severe?

People often think that an eternity in punishment is too severe. Do we really deserve eternal punishment for just a few sins? Our answer to this question reveals our view of God. God is infinitely valuable or priceless, and every sin is targeted against God. It is the difference between throwing out a painting you bought at garage sale versus trashing a painting by Michelangelo. A painting is a painting, right? No way! One is precious, the other is worthless. The value of God is so huge that any crime against him carries an infinite penalty because he is infinitely glorious.

Many people try to compensate for their sin by doing good works. They believe that if they do more good than bad God will accept them. However, Scripture teaches that no one can earn heaven. Romans 6:23 teaches that eternal life (with God in heaven) is a "gift." Do you earn a gift?

_____

_____

_____

Read Ephesians 2:8–9. The Bible teaches that salvation is by grace (undeserved kindness) through faith (trust in God). What does verse 9 say? What does it mean?

_____

_____

_____

_____

What are some things that people do to try to earn heaven?

_____

_____

_____

So far the news has been very bad. We all have sinned. Because of that sin, we deserve judgment. Further, there is nothing we can do to earn salvation. If that were the end of the story, it would be a tragic book. Thankfully, it goes on. The Bible says that God has made a way for you and all others to avoid the lake of fire. Although you deserve hell, you don't have to go there. This is great news!

Hades Is Temporary, But...

Revelation 20:14 says that Hades will one day be cast into the lake of fire. Hades is a terrible but temporary place of judgment where sinners wait for the great white throne. It could be compared to a county jail where criminals await trial. However, following the trial of sinners at the great white throne, they will be thrown, as condemned people of Hades, into the lake of fire. The lake of fire is a place of eternal torment under God's judgment. Those who go to Hades will all be moved to the lake of fire for the remainder of eternity. (In some translations "Hades" is translated as "hell"; but the English word "hell" also translates another word, "Gehenna," which is used to refer to eternal punishment, e.g., Mark 9:42–44.)

▶ You and Jesus

The Bible has much to say about who Jesus, the Son of God, is:

- He is eternal (John 1:1–2).

- He is God (John 1:1).

- He is the _____ (John 1:3).

- He (the Son) became "flesh" (John 1:14). What does "flesh" mean?

_____

_____

_____

• He is absolutely sinless (Hebrews 4:15).

Romans 5:8 teaches something else about Jesus. It says that he loves us. How did he show his love for us?

_____

_____

Most people know that Jesus died, but very few understand why he died. First Peter 3:18 answers that question:

• It says, "Christ also suffered once for sins." When did he do that?

_____

_____

• Scripture teaches that Jesus never sinned. Whose sins, then, did he die for?

_____

_____

• Christ died, "the righteous for the unrighteous." Who is the righteous one?

_____

_____

• Who are the unrighteous ones?

_____

_____

• What is the purpose and result of this substitution?
  "...that _____"

Don't miss this important point: Jesus (the righteous one) died for you (the unrighteous one). He took your place as a substitute. He paid the penalty that you deserve! Remember Romans 6:23. Because of sin, you deserve death. Instead, Jesus paid that penalty by dying on the cross! You are released from paying for your sins in the lake of fire forever, Jesus suffered death one time on Calvary. He paid for your sins!

Principle

Because of God's great love, he sent Jesus to die on the cross as your substitute.

Now look back at 1 Peter 3:18. "For Christ also suffered once for sins, the righteous for the unrighteous, _____ _____" (ESV).

That is great news! Jesus died to pay the penalty that you deserve so that you can escape punishment and gain heaven!

Guilty...But Free!

A tale is told of two brothers who immigrated to the US from China in the early 1900s. The older brother began his new life by getting a job and a house. The younger, however, was determined to enjoy his new freedom by spending his days and nights drinking and gambling. One horrible night he began fighting with a man who had accused him of cheating. In his drunken state, the younger brother drew a knife and murdered the man. He knew that if he were caught that he would be hanged. He fled to his brother's home.

The police began to search for the murderer. As the older brother entered his home, he found a pile of bloodstained clothes. Immediately, he knew what his brother had done. A few moments later, the police came to his home, only to find the older brother wearing clothes stained with blood. Throughout the questioning and trial he remained silent. He eventually died for a crime that he did not commit. He was moved by love for his brother. He died as a substitute, the innocent for the guilty. This story can help to illustrate the substitution that is enacted through Christ, but it fails to picture all that God has done through Christ when he suffered for the sinner.

Though innocent, Christ died for another's sins. Though guilty, the sinner goes free—ransomed from sin's curse by the violent death of Jesus.

▶ You and Sin

The Bible teaches that you will live somewhere forever—either in heaven or the lake of fire. Jesus died to give you access to heaven. Although some people teach that there are many ways to heaven, the Bible teaches that there is only one. Read John 14:6 to know what the only way to the Father is:

_____

_____

_____

Jesus is offering a tremendous gift: freedom from hell and eternity in heaven. Sadly, many people reject Jesus and his offer of salvation. John 1:12 instructs you to "receive" Christ instead of rejecting him. The key question is this: How can you receive Jesus Christ and his gift of salvation? There are two simultaneous aspects to receiving Christ:

1. *You must repent of your sins.*

    You have offended God by doing what you want to do. You now need to turn from selfishness and sin and submit to God's will—that is what Scripture calls *repentance*. It is not cleaning up or reforming yourself. Remember, you cannot earn heaven. Instead, repentance is changing your mind about God and sin. It is desiring to follow God's will instead of your own sinful will. C. S. Lewis puts it this way: "Fallen man is not simply an imperfect creature who needs improvement: he is a rebel who must lay down his arms…. This process of surrender is what Christians call repentance" (*Mere Christianity*, 59).

Two Different Sides of the Same Coin

Faith and repentance cannot be separated. Genuine faith includes repentance, and genuine repentance includes faith. Think of it this way...

Your Way ← God's Way

Isaiah 55:7 pictures you as a rebel who insists on going your own way, the exact opposite of God's way. It then instructs you to "forsake" your way (repentance) and "return" to the Lord (faith).

Your Way → God's Way

In order to be saved, you must turn to God and away from sin. If you have not turned from your own way, you have not turned to Christ.

What does Acts 3:19 require for your sins to be forgiven?

_____

_____

_____

First Thessalonians 1:9 defines repentance and conversion as turning "to _____, from _____."

Indeed, the very move toward Christ demands a move away from sin and idols. Christ replaces your way. He will not be merely added to a life lived in self-seeking.

According to Matthew 1:21, from what does Jesus save you?

_____

_____

Confession

Confession is the act of admission: 1) admitting that you are guilty, and 2) knowing that your sin is horrible and hating your sin (Romans 10:9–19).

There are some people who believe they are forgiven even though they have never turned from sin. They believe that they can have the best of both worlds: they can live for themselves and try to live for God too. They hope by adding a little Jesus to their life that they can go to heaven. Yet, according to Matthew 1:21, Christ saves his people from *sin*, not just the penalty in hell. Anyone who has not repented of his sin has not been saved! That is not to say that a saved man will not struggle with sin. However, a saved man has "changed his mind" about sin. He may struggle with it, but he won't continue to delight in it (1 John 3:6)

Isaiah 55:7 gives a clear picture of repentance. Explain it in your own words.

_____

_____

_____

If you have not yet turned from your wicked way, you have not yet been saved!

2. *You must trust in Jesus Christ alone.*

John 3:16, probably the most well-known verse of the Bible, teaches that you must believe in Jesus. More than just an acknowledgment that He lived and died, the Bible word *believe* means to be convinced, to trust or to place your faith in someone. You must realize that Jesus is your: (1) only hope of going to heaven and (2) only hope of being forgiven for sins. Therefore, you must trust him completely for both life and forgiveness. Trusting Jesus plus good works is insufficient. Trusting Jesus plus baptism is insufficient. Trusting Jesus plus church is insufficient. These efforts are all tainted by sin and reveal a lack of total trust in Christ. Rather, Jesus—with no help from you—gives forgiveness and life.

Individual Salvation

God promises eternal life and complete forgiveness to anyone who turns to Jesus Christ as his Lord and Savior.

In Acts 16:30, a sinful man asks the apostle Paul and Silas a vital question: "What must I do to be saved?" What was their simple answer in Acts 16:31?

_____

_____

Read John 3:36. Notice that the Bible divides all of humanity into two groups. There is no middle ground. How do the two groups respond to Christ?

_____

_____

_____

What happens to the people in each of these groups?

_____

_____

_____

What do Romans 10:9 and 13 suggest as the right response to God's saving grace? What do you have to do to be saved?

_____

_____

_____

The way to "call upon the name of the Lord" is to speak to him in prayer. The point is not that prayer saves you, but that you turn to the Lord for rescue and turn away from any other false hope, especially self-trust. If you have never trusted Jesus as your Savior, you can do it immediately—you don't need to wait any longer. Because words help us to think clearly, it would be good for you to personally express sorrow for your sin, request God's forgiveness, convey your hope in Jesus' death and resurrection, and affirm your desire to love and obey him. If you have trusted in God alone, Scripture promises that you are saved!

Many have committed to being faithful followers of Jesus Christ and have asked him to be their Savior. This passage teaches that those who have done so *know* that they will be saved from God's wrath because of the trustworthiness of God's own promises. Do you have that assurance?

Principle

Your only hope of salvation is Jesus. His death and resurrection is the only way to be saved. He died in place of the sinner. Repent and turn from selfish living and trust Jesus Christ as your personal Savior.

Once you have trusted Jesus Christ as your Savior, God begins to mature you in your relationship with Christ.

Here are some key steps in that direction:

- Although you are a Christian, you will still struggle with sin. Sin will not remove you from God's family, but it will remove you from joy and fellowship with God. Restore that open relationship by confessing sin directly to God as soon as you are aware of it. This matter will be dealt with in greater detail in the third lesson, so keep going!

- Begin reading your Bible. Start with the Gospel of Mark. Make notes of who Jesus is, what he did, and what he has done for you. The importance of immersing yourself in the Word of God will be addressed in the lesson five.

- Get involved in a church that faithfully preaches the Bible. The importance of being committed to a good, gospel-centered church will be covered in the lesson seven.

- Begin memorizing God's Word on your own. Memorizing Scripture will help you to better understand it, will prepare you to share it with others, and will help protect you from error and sin. The following section has some great verses to start with.

- Remember that turning from sin and trusting Christ for forgiveness and for power to change is not a one-time event. It should characterize your daily life (Matthew 6:11–12, 1 John 1:8–10). Expect your confidence of final salvation to grow as you continue to hold fast to Christ while enduring trials and temptations (Romans 5:1–11).

▶ Scripture Memory

John 3:16

"For God so loved the world, that he gave his only Son, that whoever believes in him should not perish but have eternal life."

Romans 6:23

"For the wages of sin is death, but the free gift of God is eternal life in Christ Jesus our Lord."

Ephesians 2:8–9

"For by grace you have been saved through faith. And this is not your own doing; it is the gift of God, not a result of works, so that no one may boast."

▶ Check Your Progress

What are the three most significant things you learned in this lesson? Why are they important?

1. _____

   _____

   _____

2. _____

   _____

   _____

3. _____

   _____

   _____

Answer the following questions to measure your understanding of salvation:

1. Two important implications arise from the fact that God created you. What are they?

   _____

   _____

   _____

2. How many people have sinned?

   _____

   _____

   _____

3. Because of your sin, what do you deserve? Be specific.

_____

_____

_____

4. What is the difference between Hades and the lake of fire?

_____

_____

_____

5. Is it possible to earn eternal life? Why or why not?

_____

_____

_____

6. In what sense was Jesus your Substitute?

_____

_____

_____

7. Why is Jesus the only way to get to the Father?

_____

_____

_____

8. What is repentance?

    _____

    _____

    _____

9. What must you do to be saved?

    _____

    _____

    _____

10. Have you personally trusted Christ? Be prepared to share your story.

    _____

    _____

    _____

Check off the following verses only when you can say them from memory:

☐ John 3:16

☐ Romans 6:23

☐ Ephesians 2:8–9

☐ Romans 10:9, 13

▶ Notes and Questions

Eternal Security

Does being a Christian mean that you will never sin again? If you commit a sin, are you still saved? Do you need to be saved again each time you sin?

One of the great blessings of the Bible is that it gives clear answers to these important questions. Time and time again the Bible teaches genuine believers are eternally secure—that is, once you are saved you cannot lose your salvation. God is not a halfway sort of God. In his great power and unchangeable purpose, he has rescued us through Christ. Nothing can keep our God from accomplishing his good purposes for us. This is the marvelous hope of every believer. Work through this study to find out what the Bible says about sin and security for the Christian.

The Bible teaches that the salvation you received at the moment you repented of your sins and trusted in Christ is irrevocable. This vital doctrine is called *eternal security*. Once you have been saved from sin by grace and through faith, you are eternally secure. You cannot be torn away from God. Eternal security is indeed a "foundational" doctrine, and it is supported by the entirety of Scripture.

A twin teaching that must not be forgotten in this study is perseverance. Perseverance is the doctrine that emphasizes the practical growth and right living of the Christian. Ignoring perseverance may lead a person to sense of safety in a profession that may not be valid. Security is what God gives to the believer; perseverance is the believer's steady progress toward a Christ-like life.[1] This lesson will focus on security that God gives to those who believe.

When you trusted Jesus Christ as your personal Savior, a lot of things changed, and they changed permanently. You were hopeless and lost before you trusted Christ, but now...

▶ You Are Saved by Grace

Ephesians 2:8–9 was discussed in Lesson 1 regarding your salvation. These verses apply also to your security. Verse 8 states that you "*have been* saved" by grace; it does not say "*were* saved by grace." The tense of the verb is present perfect, indicating that your salvation started by grace, but it also *continues* by that same grace.

---

[1] Perseverance is the doctrine that God works within us to keep us doing what is right. If we were left on our own, we would soon walk away from God. We are not left on our own. We will stay loving and obedient to God because he is at work in us. This causes us to stay committed to God so that we persevere!

Amazing Grace!

"Tis grace that brought me safe thus far, and grace will lead me home." These words from John Newton's beloved hymn proclaim the truth that just as you become saved by Christ's work, not your own, you remain saved by Christ's work, not your own.

Read Galatians 3:1–6. How did you enter God's family: by faith ("the Spirit") or by your own effort ("the flesh")?

_____

_____

How, then, will you stay in God's family and grow as a Christian: by faith or by your own effort?

_____

_____

Read John 1:12–13. What right (privilege or ability) did Jesus give you when you believed in him as your Lord and Savior?

_____

_____

What type of birth must you experience in order to enter Christ's kingdom (John 3:5–6, 8)?

_____

_____

Nicodemus had a good question in this passage: How can a man be born twice? Jesus explained what it means to be "born again" in John

3:5–7. Your first birth was physical. When did that physical birth happen?[2]

_____

_____

Your second birth is spiritual. When did that happen?

_____

_____

When you received Jesus Christ, you became a child of God—you were born into his family! God is your heavenly Father! Is a normal parent-child relationship temporary or permanent?

_____

_____

Once you become God's child, you are his child forever. Here's an illustration:[3]

As you grew up, did you ever make your father or mother angry by disobeying them?

_____

_____

---

[2] When Jesus says the word *again* he uses a term that has two definitions. It is the same word for "from above" (i.e., from heaven). Nicodemus misunderstands Jesus and asks about a repeat, physical birth. Jesus was speaking about a heavenly birth, not a being born again like a baby.

[3] In reality this graph is too simple, but it helps to illustrate that our relationship with God is unbreakable and permanent. However, the Bible also explains that a healthy Christian will experience deeper and closer fellowship with God over the course of his life. When we are inside the "fellowship box" in this picture, we are increasing in our fellowship with God, growing in grace; when we are outside the fellowship box, we are decreasing in fellowship with God and regressing toward worldliness. Fellowship is a dynamic idea; it's either growing or shrinking. Still, those who have truly trusted Christ and followed him as Lord have a secure relationship with him as this graph illustrates. God will preserve them, and thus, they will persevere in faith, love, and holiness. See Lesson 3 for more.

When you did, were you still their child?

_____

_____

You still had a relationship with them—you didn't have to go to the courthouse downtown and become adopted! You are their child regardless of what you do. Your *relationship* was unchanged, but your *fellowship* was broken—you weren't as close as you had been. The same is true of your relationship with your heavenly Father. When you sin, you are still his child— that's your *relationship*. Because Christ is our substitute, we have a status of 100 percent righteous before God. But you are not as close to him when you sin—that's your broken *fellowship*. Because sin is present with us, we have varying experience of closeness to God.

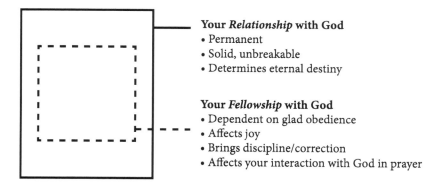

Your *Relationship* with God
- Permanent
- Solid, unbreakable
- Determines eternal destiny

Your *Fellowship* with God
- Dependent on glad obedience
- Affects joy
- Brings discipline/correction
- Affects your interaction with God in prayer

You have a relationship with God—you became part of his family the moment you were saved. You are secure in him! Though your sin hurts your fellowship with God, your relationship is eternal and unchanging.

▶ You Are in Christ

The Bible teaches that when you trust Jesus as your Savior you gain a new position: you are *in Christ*. You become joined to Jesus Christ (Col. 3:3). Since you are in Christ, you have the position and privileges before God that Jesus earned as your human representative!

Romans 8:1 says that since you are "in Christ" you will not face _____. That means that you will not be punished for your sins because Christ already paid for the sins of his people!

Colossians 2:13 says that you were dead in your trespasses before salvation. But then the verse goes on to speak of something that God did for you in Christ. What did he do?

_____

_____

Second Corinthians 5:17 says, "If anyone is in Christ, he is a _____ _____."

The second half of the verse lists two practical results of your new birth. What are they?

1. _____

2. _____

As Good as Done!

Romans 8:30 uses several words to describe God's work of salvation on your behalf. One of them is *glorified*, which describes the condition of those in heaven who are free from sin, disease, and death. The verse says that God has already glorified you (past tense). In other words, in God's eyes your salvation and glorification in heaven are so certain that he describes it as already having occurred! You are eternally secure!

Romans 5:1 says that when you put your faith in Christ as your Savior you were "justified." That means that from that moment onward God views you as righteous and treats you as though you are righteous.

Romans 4:11, 23–24 teaches that at the moment of salvation, God imputes Jesus' righteousness to us—which means that God thinks of Christ's righteousness as belonging to us. Although you continue to struggle with sin (in your practice), God now sees you as being as righteous as Jesus Christ (in your standing). Why? Because you are in Christ!

Our own judicial system operates in a similar way. Take, for example, a person who is declared guilty by the judge but in reality he is innocent. Though he is innocent, the court and our government will treat him as though he is *truly* guilty based on the declaration of the judge. We also know that sometimes the court declares a person innocent when in fact he is guilty. How does the court treat this person? Does he pay for his crime even though he has been declared innocent? Certainly not. God, in his courtroom, has condemned the innocent Christ as guilty and declared the repentant sinner to be innocent instead. This is the verdict that Jesus gladly secured for you when he died on the cross (we call this a substitution or substitutionary atonement).

▶ You Are Kept by the Power of God

Throughout church history, the matter of eternal security has been addressed from two different perspectives:

1. Perseverance

Perseverance is the teaching that genuine believers will all persevere; the believer will continue to live by faith in God. Read 1 John 2:19. It teaches that those who fail to "persevere" do not *lose* their salvation. Rather, they prove that they never were believers in the first place.

2. Preservation

Preservation is the other side of the coin in this issue of security. Its focus is not on the Christian, but on God himself. It is the teaching that God will preserve all who are genuinely saved. According to 1 Peter 1:5, you do not keep your salvation by human effort. Rather you are guarded "by _____'s _____." We persevere because God is faithfully working in us, preserving us.

Read John 6:37–40. Christ teaches that he will not lose any that the Father has given him. Also read Jude 24. It teaches that God is "able to _____ you from _____, and to present you blameless" in heaven. The question is not whether you could lose your salvation; it is whether God could lose you!

Were it up to you to keep yourself saved, you would be in trouble! Thankfully, God has given Christ the responsibility of "keeping" you. Because of this, you are perfectly secure!

Read John 10:27–29. In verse 27, what does Jesus call those who have received him as their Savior?

_____

_____

How do saved people reveal that they belong to their Shepherd (v. 27)?

_____

_____

Jesus gives three promises in v. 28. What are they?

1. _____

2. _____

3. _____

What promise does Jesus repeat in v. 29?

_____

_____

Is God able to keep you? _____ Is He willing? _____

What important promise did Jesus make in John 6:37?

_____

_____

▶ You Are in God's Love

Romans 8:35–39 are comforting verses for the Christian. What question is asked in v. 35?

_____

_____

What difficulties are mentioned in vv. 35–36?

_____

_____

What answer is given in v. 37? [ANSWER LINE(S)]

_____

_____

List all of the things in vv. 38–39 that cannot separate us from God's love.

_____

_____

_____

Jeremiah 31:3 describes God's love as "everlasting." What does that mean?

_____

_____

_____

Can you lose your salvation? Only if God stops loving you, but Scripture says that is impossible.

▶ God's Spirit Is in You

The Bible teaches that Christians are saved by grace, are adopted into God's family, are placed in Christ, are kept by the power of God, and cannot be separated from his love. Scripture also teaches that God is in you! Read 1 Corinthians 6:19. What does it call you?

_____

_____

In the Old Testament, God lived in the tabernacle (a portable, tent-like place of worship). He later lived in the temple, the permanent place of worship in Jerusalem. Of course, God is everywhere (omnipresent), but the tabernacle and temple were his special dwelling places among his people. Now, God's special dwelling place is in his people, including you!

Some people believe that the Holy Spirit lives only in obedient Christians, but the Bible teaches that he lives in all Christians. Read 1 Corinthians 3:1. How does God describe the people in the church of Corinth?

_____

_____

_____

Though saved, the Corinthian Christians were disobedient, living for their own sinful desires ("people of the flesh"). Yet, just a few chapters later, God calls the believer a "temple of the Holy Spirit" (1 Cor. 6:19). Do you lose the Holy Spirit and your salvation when you sin?

_____

_____

Read Ephesians 1:13–14. Verse 14 says that the Holy Spirit is the "guarantee of our inheritance." When you purchase a home you put down a deposit of money. What does this signify?

_____

_____

_____

In the same way, God gave his Spirit to you as a guarantee; it is his promise that he will complete the transaction. You are assured that your eternity in heaven (inheritance) is settled. In fact, Ephesians 4:30 says that you have been "sealed" by the Spirit until you are redeemed. A seal was used to protect the contents of a letter from damage or tampering; you are secured from damage or loss by the Spirit. However, when you choose to sin there are consequences. Even though God's Spirit does not leave, he does respond. How so (Ephesians 4:30)?

_____

_____

_____

▶ God's Life Is in You

Throughout Scripture God promises life to those who have received Jesus Christ as their personal Savior. Have you repented of your sin and asked Jesus to be your Savior?

_____

_____

FOUNDATIONS

If so, John 5:24 is one of God's many promises to you. What does it promise?

_____

_____

According to Scripture, those who trust in Christ have eternal life (John 3:16, 36). Eternal life does not become yours when you die; it is currently your possession if you've trusted Christ.

This point is an important safeguard of the doctrine of eternal security. Some who criticize this teaching argue that it might lead to a life of sin because the Christian has no fear of losing his salvation. Such belief that eternal security is "dangerous" is based in human logic, not Scripture. Charles Spurgeon responded to this type of groundless charge by saying, "The question is, is it in the Bible? If it is there let none of us ever say it is dangerous."[4]

▶ You Are a New Creature

In 2 Corinthians 5:17, Paul states that the Christian is a "_____
_____." The results of the new birth are evident in everyday life as "the old has passed away; behold, the _____ has come." A genuine believer should not want to sin! He ought to live as a new person who has been set free from sin. Does *your* life demonstrate that kind of change?

_____

_____

_____

_____

_____

[4] Charles Haddon Spurgeon, *Spurgeon's Sermons* (Grand Rapids: Baker Books, 1999), vol. X. However, there are some so-called believers who are not believers, but simply desire to claim the hope of heaven without claiming the Savior of heaven. These people are not saved. First John was written to give tests of living faith to help those struggling with this question.

41

It is true that there are some who claim to be saved, and yet continue to enjoy sin without any sorrow for sin.

What about them? First John 1:6 provides the answer: "If we say we have fellowship with [God] while we walk in darkness, we lie and do not practice the truth" (see also 1 John 3:10). You cannot claim to have fellowship with God (i.e., claim to be saved), and yet continue to live in unrepentant sin! Those who continue in sin with no sign of "new creature" living are not really saved, nor were they ever saved.

Scripture teaches that true believers are truly secure in Christ—secure to obey, not to sin. The true believer walks in obedience, motivated by a loyal love for his Savior. This commitment is life-changing!

Moved by Love

"There is nothing like a belief in my eternal perseverance, and the immutability of my Father's affection, which can keep me near to Him from a motive of simple gratitude." (Spurgeon, "A Defense of Calvinism, in *A Great Heritage of Evangelical Teaching*, 928). This truth is proven throughout church history. Many of the most devout Christians—from the apostle Paul to the Puritans—believed fully in the security of the believer.

▶ Fact, Faith, and Feeling

There may be times when you don't feel assured of your salvation. Such lack of assurance[5] may be caused by sin which you've allowed

---

[5] It is important to distinguish the objective and unchanging security of the believer with subjective assurance of salvation. Assurance refers to your confidence and certainty that you

to be part of your life. Or it may be Satan's attempts to discourage you. Whatever the cause of doubt, you must remember that your salvation is not dependent on how you feel or how you perform. It is based on the finished work of Christ. Your responsibility is to turn to God in faith based on the promises of his Word, all the while fighting sin and pursuing holiness (2 Peter 1:5–10). The fact is that a person is saved by God's grace through faith. As a believer, you are now in God's family. You are in Christ. God holds you. His Spirit and life are in you. You are a new creature. God has promised that he won't cast you out.

What do we learn about God from Titus 1:2?

_____

_____

_____

How does that description of God prove you cannot lose your salvation?

_____

_____

_____

The belief that you can lose your salvation—a belief held as part of Arminianism—is not a minor issue. It is believed by millions. Its implications for individuals are obvious. However, its implications for Bible doctrine are also great. The stakes are very high. Doctrine does matter:

---

are saved. Assurance of salvation is important and grounded in Scriptural teaching (such as Romans 8:16), security is based on an objective promise—God saves all who believe.

1. *This false teaching has a low view of salvation.*

    It teaches that you receive eternal life by grace, but keep it by works (contrary to Galatians 3:2–3). In the end, it amounts to works salvation. The result of such teaching is the pride condemned in Ephesians 2:9 and a false faith placed on the sinner rather than the Savior. One of the greatest hopes of the believer is that Jesus has done it all, we do nothing to be saved!

2. *This false teaching has a low view of sin.*

    Many who teach that you lose your salvation by sin also teach —of necessity—that it is possible to live a life entirely free from sin (contrary to all of Scripture and the experience of the apostle Paul in Romans 7). To justify the belief that one can be sinless, they often redefine or minimize sin. They boast of not being drunkards, adulterers or liars, but they neglect sins of the heart such as anger, pride, and lust. No one who correctly understands God's holiness would presume to be called sinless (1 John 1:8–10).

3. *This false teaching has a low view of God.*

    It teaches that God would bestow a gift, then change his mind (contrary to Romans 11:29). It teaches that he would exact punishment for one sinner two times (contrary to Hebrews 1:3 and 1 Peter 3:18). It makes God erratic.

    Read Malachi 3:6. Here God states the reason why he did not "consume" (or destroy) Israel, though they certainly deserved it. What reason does he give for his continuing mercy? "For I the LORD, _____."

    God's preservation of his people had more to do with his character than his people's. Similarly, your security as a Christian does not rest in your performance. Instead, it rests in the unchanging Word and character of God. What a great truth, no matter what you as a believer do, God will not love you less. You are safe, forever!

4. *This false teaching has a low view of Christ.*

It teaches that, although he died for sin, his death is inadequate to pay for all sins (contrary to 1 John 1:7) and insufficient to satisfy God's justice (contrary to 1 John 2:1–2 and Isaiah 53:11).

John 19:30 tells of Christ's sixth cry from the cross. It was a declaration of victory: "It is _____!" That glorious phrase comes from one single Greek word: *tetelestai*. It is a word used to describe a payment or purchase where it means that the account in question has been "paid in full." When Christ uttered those words from the cross, he proclaimed that he paid your sins fully. No more payment is required. It is finished. For God to require two payments (one by Christ and one by you) would be unjust.

Consider this: when Christ died for your sins nearly 2000 years ago, how many sins had you committed? All of your sins were yet in the future, including those you committed yesterday, today, and even tomorrow. Yet, according to 1 John 1:7, how many of them are washed away by Christ's blood (even those you have not yet done)?

_____

_____

In the words of Charles Wesley, "Love's redeeming work is done, Hallelujah! Fought the fight, the battle won, Hallelujah!"

Finally, 1 John 2:1 contains a very strong proof of eternal security, and it is found in the person and work of Jesus Christ. Although God's desires that you "sin not," he has also provided an "advocate" or representative for us when we do sin. Who is it?

_____

_____

Furthermore, Christ is called the "propitiation" for our sins in v. 2. (Propitiation is a complete removal of God's anger over sinful behavior.) That means that Jesus has satisfied God's wrath against us by dying on the cross. As stated earlier, Christ suffered our punishment/God's anger even for those sins that we have not yet committed. That is amazing grace!

▶ Conclusion

It is essential that you become fully convinced of your security in Christ. Be certain that you have indeed trusted Christ. "Grow in the grace and knowledge of our Lord and Savior Jesus Christ" (2 Peter 3:18). Make sure that your lifestyle indicates the change befitting a "new creation" (cf. 2 Corinthians 5:17). Compare your life with the tests of salvation listed in 1 John. In the words of 2 Peter 1:10, "be all the more diligent to confirm your calling and election." Lewis Sperry Chafer provides this warning: the Bible offers "no divine promise of keeping for the mere professor who does not truly believe" (*Salvation*, 71).

Once you have placed your faith in Christ alone, do not be anxious about his ability to save you. As long as you doubt God's power to give you salvation, your insecurity will hurt your ability to grow or serve. Take God at his word and stand secure in the promise of 1 Peter 1:5—you are "kept by the power of God" (NKJV). Move past your doubts and get busy!

If you still struggle with whether you are really saved, then revisit Lesson 1 and see if that helps you to understand who is qualified to have this type of security. Also, talk about your doubts with a spiritual mentor. The problem is never whether God is able to save someone, but whether someone is really a recipient of his grace.

Remember, sin does not destroy a Christian's relationship with God. However, sin does bring distance in your fellowship with God. Lesson 3 will discuss growing in your fellowship with God.

Secure to Serve

During the early stages of the construction of the Golden Gate Bridge no safety devices were used and construction was slow because of the fear of falling—usually to one's death. However, for the final part of the project a large safety net was suspended under the workers. Nineteen men fell into it and were saved from almost certain death. Even more interesting, however, is the fact that significantly more work was accomplished after the net was installed. Why? Because men felt security—they were free to work without fear.

▶ Scripture Memory

John 6:37

"All that the Father gives me will come to me, and whoever comes to me I will never cast out."

John 10:27–29

"My sheep hear my voice, and I know them, and they follow me. I give them eternal life, and they will never perish, and no one will snatch them out of my hand. My Father, who has given them to me, is greater than all, and no one is able to snatch them out of the Father's hand."

1 John 2:1

"My little children, I am writing these things to you so that you may not sin. But if anyone does sin, we have an advocate with the Father, Jesus Christ the righteous."

▶ Check Your Progress

What are the three most significant things you learned in this lesson? Why are they important?

1. _____

_____

_____

2. _____

_____

_____

3. _____

_____

_____

Answer the following questions to measure your understanding of eternal security:

1. Why does being saved by grace mean you are eternally secure?

    _____

    _____

    _____

2. Do you continue in your Christian effort without faith?

    _____

    _____

    _____

3. What is the difference between relationship and fellowship?

    _____

    _____

    _____

4. What can separate you from the love of God?

    _____

    _____

    _____

5. Is it possible to be struggling with sin and yet be saved?

    _____

    _____

    _____

6. When does eternal life begin?

_____

_____

_____

7. What motivates Christian obedience?

_____

_____

_____

8. What is the difference between security and assurance?

_____

_____

_____

9. If it were possible to lose salvation by sinning, who would remain saved?

_____

_____

_____

Check off the following verses only when you can say them from memory:

☐ John 6:37

☐ John 10:27–29

☐ 1 John 2:1

▶ **Notes and Questions**

CONFESSION OF SIN

▶ Introduction

Lesson 2 emphasized your relationship with God. Remember, once you receive Jesus Christ as your personal Savior, you are a child of God—your relationship with him cannot be broken.

This lesson will emphasize your ongoing fellowship with God over the course of your Christian life. The New Oxford American Dictionary defines fellowship as "friendly association, especially with people who share one's interests." The Greek word, *koinōnia*, can be translated, "partnership." The idea of sharing is understood in both. Although you cannot lose your salvation, sin can certainly damage your fellowship with God. Look again at the difference between your fellowship and relationship with God:

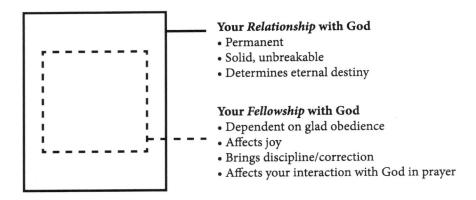

Your *Relationship* with God
- Permanent
- Solid, unbreakable
- Determines eternal destiny

Your *Fellowship* with God
- Dependent on glad obedience
- Affects joy
- Brings discipline/correction
- Affects your interaction with God in prayer

Because our *experience* of fellowship with God is always either growing or shrinking, while our *status* before God is always complete in Christ, we might look at the above concepts from a different angle. The chart below illustrates how, over the course of our Christian life, we grow in our experience of our justified status before God.

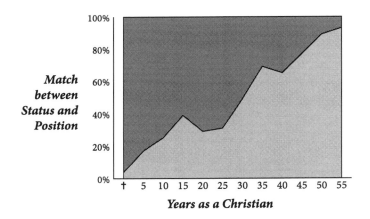

Match between Status and Position

Years as a Christian

Your Relationship with God
Permanent
Constant
Solid
Unbreakable
Grounded in Christ
Determines Eternal Destiny

Your Fellowship with God
Testifies to the Relationship
Changeable
Dependent on Glad Obedience
Brings Assurance and Joy
Warns of Discipline and Correction
Determines Effectiveness of Prayer
Fulfilled When We See Christ

The more mature you become as a Christian, the more certain will be your experience of your right standing before God.

▶ Committing Sin

Read 1 John 2:1a.[1] What is God's desire regarding you and sin?

_____

_____

According to the second part of this verse and 1 John 2:2[2], God makes a provision—a "plan B"—for when you do sin. What is it?

_____

_____

What does 1 John 1:8 say about a person—Christian or non-Christian—who claims to be without sin?

_____

_____

Do not make light of sin. Although Scripture teaches that you will still struggle with sin, it also indicates that as your fellowship with Christ increases you will begin to sin less.

---

[1] An _a_ after a verse reference means the first part of a verse, and a _b_ means the second part, and so on.

[2] An advocate is someone who comes "alongside" to help or defend you. _Propitiation_ is a sacrifice that puts God's anger to rest; Jesus satisfied God's wrath on your sins by dying for you. Return to Lesson 2 for more on propitiation.

Read 2 Corinthians 5:17. What does the Bible call someone who is saved (someone who is "in Christ")?

_____

_____

Describe the last part of this verse in your own words.

_____

_____

_____

What was the desire of John in 1 John 2:1?

_____

_____

Someone who genuinely has been saved is a different person. In 1 Corinthians 6:9–11, Paul was writing to Christians in Corinth. What sins were they doing before they were saved? (Note: The key word is *were*.)

_____

_____

_____

What does the Bible say happened to them when they were saved?

_____

_____

As a Christian you will still struggle with sin—key word, *struggle*. If you do not care that you sin, and you do not battle the tendency to sin, then the Bible would say that you have never been saved! You will inevitably follow your own desires and the influences around which will lead you away from God. See 1 John 3:4–10.[3]

▶ Consequences of Sin

The Bible teaches that you will need to struggle against sin until your death (1 John 1:8–10; Romans 7:14–25). How to win battles with temptation will be covered in a later section. A believer who loses the battle with temptation and sins, is still saved. However, there are some dire consequences of sin.

The first consequence when you sin is that you offend God. What did David say about his sin in Psalm 51:4a?

_____

_____

_____

What does 1 John 1:5 teach about God and sin?

_____

_____

Why is God offended by sin? Sin is not just breaking a rule; it is breaking *God's* rule. How does 1 John 3:4 define sin?

_____

_____

The New Testament refers to the law as the "law of Christ" (1 Corinthians 9:21) based on God's goal that we be like Jesus Christ.

---

[3] The Greek verbs in this passage are present tense. They indicate a continual action or state of being: commits, does, sins, and so on. The ESV says it well, "makes a practice of sinning." This letter by John is addressing continuous, habitual sinning, and not the normal struggle to stop sinning that is common to all Christians.

A second serious consequence of sin is revealed in Psalm 66:18. What is it?

_____

_____

The *Holman Christian Standard Bible* (HCSB) translates Isaiah 59:2, "But your iniquities have built barriers between you and your God, and your sins have made him hide his face from you so that He does not listen." As was stated earlier, a Christian's sin weakens his fellowship with God—like a wall has been built between you and God, your sins pile up like bricks. Sin deadens a believer to God's priorities. You don't need to be saved again, but you do need to strengthen your fellowship with him. A child who disobeys his parent is still part of the family, but the association and communication among the family is hindered until the child confesses his disobedience.

▶ Discipline for Sin

Yet another consequence of sin is discipline. Hebrews 12:5–11 is the classic passage on God's discipline of those he loves.

Read Hebrews 12:5–7. What human relationship parallels our relationship with God?

_____

_____

According to v. 6, what emotion motivates God's discipline?

_____

_____

Explain the above answer. How can discipline be loving?

_____

_____

Read verses 7–8. What is true of a person's relationship to God if he continues in sin but is never disciplined for his sin?

_____

_____

Verse 8 makes sense. You may discipline your own child for disobedience, but you don't discipline a stranger's child for doing the same thing. God's discipline confirms that you are indeed God's child and is an crucial test of genuine salvation.

Read Hebrews 12:9–11. God does not discipline us pointlessly, but for our good. Verses 10 and 11 each give some purposes for God's chastening. What are his goals?

_____

_____

_____

▶ Conviction of Sin

The word *conviction* means "proof of sin." Conviction is the work of the Holy Spirit in the heart of someone who has sinned. The Spirit convinces you of your sin. According to Ephesians 4:30, how does your sin affect the Holy Spirit?

_____

_____

What does that mean, and why should it motivate you to avoid sin?

_____

_____

_____

You can be sure of this: when you sin and grieve the Holy Spirit, he will not sit idly by and allow you to destroy yourself. He makes you uncomfortable about what you have done. One of the clearest instances of such conviction in the Bible comes from King David in Psalm 32. In the first two verses he speaks of the happiness (*blessedness*) of someone who has had his sins forgiven. Why does he state that forgiveness brings happiness? He knows by experience that sin brings misery to a believer's heart until it is confessed and forgiven. How did David describe the Holy Spirit's conviction of sin in Psalm 32:3–4?

_____

_____

David was sick from guilt, but he eventually responded to conviction by confessing his sin (Psalm 32:5).

No Stone Unturned

David obviously took time for introspection, meditation, thinking, or searching his heart for sin that he had not confessed. He also acknowledged the possibility that he had sinned in ways that were unknown to him. He asked God to deal with the sin of which he was unaware. Notice his prayer in Psalm 139:23–24: "Search me, O God, and know my heart! Try me and know my thoughts! And see if there be any grievous way in me, and lead me in the way everlasting!" Our desire for purity and forgiveness should cause us to ask God to examine us, leaving no stone unturned so that we can confess our sins to our Savior.

Sometimes Christians are confused when they continue to feel guilty after they have confessed their sin to God. While they are working diligently to make things right and live obediently, they may assume that these guilty feelings are evidence that God has not forgiven them yet. It will be helpful to examine the difference between *conviction* and *condemnation*. Perhaps you have experienced a feeling of guilt when you have sinned. If so, you are experiencing God's conviction. This conviction will continue until you "confess and forsake" your sin (Proverbs 28:13). However, if that feeling of guilt lingers even after you have confessed and forsaken your sin, it is no longer a work of God's Spirit. It is condemnation.

Satan wants forgiven Christians to feel guilty so that they will be useless for the Lord. What is Satan called in Revelation 12:10?

_____

_____

Satan not only accuses you before God; he also accuses you to yourself. He wants you to doubt God's forgiveness. He delights in reminding you of sin and making you feel condemned. Thankfully, Jesus is our advocate and answers the accuser on our behalf (1 John 2:1).

Conviction

- Conviction is a work of God.

- Conviction urges you to return to God and be forgiven for your sin: "You sinned again, but Christ paid for that sin. Confess it and return to fellowship with him."

- Conviction ends the moment you confess your sin to God. It will never be brought up again.

Condemnation

- Condemnation is a work of Satan.

- Condemnation urges you to give up your walk with God: "You're a failure. You call yourself a Christian? You tried and failed. Just quit. God couldn't forgive you again."

- Condemnation continues even after you've confessed your sin to God. Satan delights in reminding you of past sins.

In your own words, summarize the difference between conviction and condemnation?

_____

_____

_____

▶ Confession of Sin

What condition and promise does God give to Christians in 1 John 1:9?

_____

_____

_____

_____

The word _confess_ means to agree with God about your sin—that means we must hate it—and acknowledge guilt. Many people believe that confession is something done before a priest. However, biblical confession is a matter between the sinner and God alone. Look at David's definition of confession in Psalm 32:5. What does he say?

_____

_____

_____

_____

What is the opposite of confession from this verse?

_____

_____

_____

_____

To whom did David "acknowledge" his sin?

_____

_____

_____

Another verse which deals with confession of sin is Proverbs 28:13. What does it promise to someone who confesses and renounces his/her sin?

_____

_____

_____

Contrast the previous answer to David's experience in Psalm 32:3–4.

_____

_____

_____

Back to Proverbs 28:13, what two things does someone need to do in order to "obtain mercy"?

1. _____

2. _____

You know what the word *confess* means. What about the second word, *forsake*? What does it mean? Why is it necessary to forsake your transgressions?

_____

_____

_____

_____

No Middle Man!

The word *confess* may cause you to think of going to church to confess your sins to a priest. Yet, the Bible says that the believer can go directly to God as he confidently enters God's throne room (Hebrews 4, 10). We do not go to a church or priest to get forgiveness because:

- You sinned against God, not the church or priest (Psalm 51:4).

- Only God can forgive your sins (Mark 2:7).

- You don't need another "go-between" except for Jesus. In the words of 1 Timothy 2:5, "There is one mediator between God and men, the man Christ Jesus."

Compare the end of Proverbs 28:13 with Psalm 32:3–5. What is God's promise to the person who confesses sin to him?

_____

_____

_____

_____

God has said that your sin will hinder your fellowship with him until it is confessed. With that in mind, *sin should be confessed immediately and specifically.*

Confess Your Sins, Not Just Your Sin

Many Christians are content to offer blanket confessions, asking the Lord to forgive them "if they have sinned." Yet, Scripture encourages us to confess our "sins" (1 John 1:9), not just our sin. Here is a good rule to apply: Be as specific when you confess your sin as you were when you committed the sin. Deal with your failures individually as soon as you become aware of them. Only after we have made an honest confession of what sins we know about, can we ask God with integrity to cleanse us from hidden faults (Psalm 19:12).

What does God promise about forgiven sin in Hebrews 10:17?

_____

_____

What does God say about forgiven sin in Micah 7:18–19?

_____

_____

Read Psalm 103:8–14. How do these verses describe God?

_____

_____

What does God say about forgiven sin in Psalm 103:12?

_____

_____

How is God described in Psalm 86:5?

_____

_____

_____

The last several verses teach that God is *eager* to forgive you when you sin. Sadly, many Christians are slow to confess their sin and, therefore, they have inconsistent growth in their fellowship with God. Confess your sin as soon as you become aware of it. Do not let unconfessed sins accumulate. Rather, make it a life pattern to "keep short sin accounts with God." The cleansing and refreshing joy of God's forgiveness is truly a blessing for the believer!

Let's review the facts from Scripture. Although you are a Christian, you still have a leftover part of your sinful nature—you were born with a desire to sin, and that desire continues in you until your death. Sin won't remove you from God's family (your relationship), but it will sour your fellowship with him. When you find yourself grieving the Holy Spirit, leaving behind your fellowship with God, confess that sin to God immediately and specifically. Turn from that sin. God will then forgive you, and your fellowship with him will begin to grow again. True forgiveness *always* results in reconciliation; this becomes the pattern for our forgiveness of others, too.

"Among those who walk with God, there is no greater motive and incentive unto universal holiness, and the preserving of their hearts and spirits in all purity and cleanness, than this, that the blessed Spirit, who hath undertaken to dwell in them, is continually considering what they give entertainment in their hearts unto, and rejoiceth when his temple is kept undefiled."

—John Owen, *Mortification of Sin*

▶ Scripture Memory

Psalm 66:18

If I had cherished iniquity in my heart, the Lord would not have listened.

Proverbs 28:13

Whoever conceals his transgressions will not prosper, but he who confesses and forsakes them will obtain mercy.

1 John 1:9

If we confess our sins, he is faithful and just to forgive us our sins and to cleanse us from all unrighteousness.

▶ Check Your Progress

What are the three most significant things you learned in this lesson? Why are they important?

1. _____

_____

_____

2. _____

_____

_____

3. _____

_____

_____

Answer the following questions to measure your understanding of confession of sin:

1. What is God's desire concerning you and sin?

    _____

    _____

    _____

2. What provision has God made for when you sin?

    _____

    _____

    _____

3. What are some of the consequences of sin for a Christian?

    _____

    _____

    _____

4. Why does God discipline Christians?

    _____

    _____

    _____

5. What is the difference between God's conviction and Satan's condemnation?

    _____

    _____

    _____

6. Why do you confess your sins to God and not men?

   _____

   _____

   _____

7. Does God hold confessed and forgiven sins against you?

   _____

   _____

   _____

8. What specific sins is God convicting you about? Take time now to confess and forsake them.

Check off the following verses only when you can say them from memory:

☐ Psalm 66:18

☐ 1 John 1:9

☐ Proverbs 28:13

► **Notes and Questions**

LESSON 4

BAPTISM AND
THE LORD'S SUPPER

▶ **Introduction**

Baptism and communion, the two ordinances[1] of the church, are precious parts of a Christian's worship. Both offer a tremendous opportunity to display and celebrate the gospel in a public, visible way. When observed in accordance with the Scriptures, they are a testimony and proclamation of what the Lord Jesus has accomplished by saving sinners through his death. Yet, both are often misunderstood resulting in unnecessary confusion or even

---

[1] Baptism and the Lord's Supper are referred to as the two "ordinances" of the church because they were ordained by Christ as a memorial of his work on the cross.

grave error. As with other topics, our desire is to discover and follow what the Bible teaches about these two important activities.

▶ Part 1: Baptism

The Meaning of Baptism

Baptism is the term used to describe the Christian rite of initiation. It is a ceremony involving water that publically affiliates a person with Christianity. The word *baptize* belongs in a family of words used by first-century clothiers to refer to the process of dyeing cloth. When a white cloth is immersed into a red dye, the cloth goes into the dye and the dye soaks the cloth. It is used for all sorts of things getting put into something else. The Scriptures teach that baptism is immersion into water and that it is only properly applied to believers. It is a public announcement telling others that you believe and follow Jesus Christ!

The Purpose of Baptism

1. *Baptism was commanded by Jesus Christ.*

   The primary reason for being baptized is that Christ commanded it. Every Christian needs to be baptized in obedience to Jesus Christ.

   Read Matthew 28:19–20. After assuming that his hearers will "go," what three commands did Christ give his disciples in these verses?

   _____

   _____

   _____

The word sometimes translated "teach" in the first command literally means "to make disciples." The order of the three commands is important. Notice that baptism immediately follows making disciples; its position indicates that baptism is of primary importance in following Christ. Thus baptism should follow very closely the decision to follow Christ. Baptism is the first step of obedience a new Christian should take.

This last instruction by Jesus is given to the church. It is the church that is responsible for reaching the lost, baptizing new converts, and for strengthening the believer. No individual could or should try to accomplish this in isolation from his local church. This set of commands is called the Great Commission. It is the joy of each local assembly to have such clear and simple instructions for pleasing our Lord.

2. *Baptism shows that you identify with Jesus Christ.*

Baptism pictures the Christian's relationship to the gospel. Read Romans 6:1–7. Verses 3–5 teach that when we were saved by Christ we took part in his death, burial and resurrection. We are spiritually dead to sin, yet alive to "walk in newness of life" (v. 4). This truth is pictured by water baptism. Being completely submerged into water pictures Christ's death and burial, and shows our death to sin. Emerging from the water pictures Christ's resurrection and our new life. Just as Jesus died, was buried, and rose again, so every believer is dead to sin and alive to God. God has given us a way to picture the gospel, preaching it through the rich symbolism of water baptism!

Water baptism is an outward symbol of an inward reality. Our immersion into water pictures our immersion into Chris. Read Galatians 3:27. Water baptism shows what happened the moment you were saved.

Water baptism follows salvation and symbolizes the unification of believers with the Lord's death. This unity is so tight that Paul can say in Galatians 2:20 that he has been crucified with Christ!

If we have been united with Jesus in his death, as baptism pictures, what can we be certain we will also experience because we are united with him?

_____

_____

_____

3. *Baptism is your testimony for Jesus Christ.*

Another important reason FOR being baptized is that it is a public statement of your salvation. In addition to picturing the story of the gospel in general, it is a way of telling others that you have trusted Christ as your Savior. This is why baptism in the Bible was often a very public event (e.g., Matthew 3:6).

Those who are preparing to be baptized should take seriously the importance of what they are doing and, if they will have an opportunity to describe how they came to trust in Christ as Savior, pray about what they will say. If you are afforded such an opportunity, do it, and pray for the Lord to use your testimony. Many people have come to know Jesus Christ as their Savior as a result of seeing the baptism of a friend or family member. Your act of obedience may be an opportunity to give the gospel to someone who needs Christ!

4. *Baptism shows that you identify with the Body of Christ.*

In Matthew 28:19–20, the church is commanded, "Go therefore and make disciples of all nations, baptizing them in the name of the Father and of the Son and of the Holy Spirit, teaching them to observe all that I have commanded you." Baptism is part of an *initiation* into a community of disciples where you are instructed, shepherded, encouraged, and given an opportunity to participate in the corporate worship of Christ. This community of disciples is the local church. This commision can only be accomplished by the church, and baptism should only be done by the church.

The command of Matthew 28:19–20 is reflected in the obedience of the early NT church in Acts 2:41–42. There we see the clear order again: becoming a disciple, baptism, and formal identification with a local community of believers. Christian baptism has a gospel-centered meaning and testifies to faith in Christ's redemptive work; it also had a corporate dimension and declared solidarity or rich unity with others who have also trusted Christ—your local assembly. Thus, baptism is rightly connected with formal church membership as you express unity with Christ and his people.

The Prerequisite for Baptism

We have learned that it is important to obey Christ by being baptized, but let's review when it should take place. Look again at Acts 16:22–34.

After believing in the Lord Jesus Christ as instructed by Paul and Silas, what happened to the people of the jailer's household?

_____

_____

_____

Baptism immediately follows salvation by faith in Jesus Christ. As we have noted, the same sequence is seen in Matthew 28:19–20 and Acts 2:41.

For valid baptism, each person must have saving faith and should be baptized by a local assembly (or its representative, e.g., a missionary). These are all that is required.

Normally we do not study what something "is not." However, because of common problems with baptism we think it might be helpful to briefly outline what God has Before we study what baptism does accomplish, let us look at what it does not accomplish.

1. *Baptism does not save you.*

Read Acts 16:16–34, the record of the salvation of a jailer in the city of Philippi. Verses 30–33 are the important verses for this lesson.

What was the jailer's question (v. 30)?

_____

_____

_____

What answer did Paul and Silas give (v. 31)?

_____

_____

_____

In Lesson 1 you learned that the word *believe* in the New Testament means "to place faith in someone." Paul told the jailer that there is one thing necessary for salvation: faith in Jesus Christ. Notice that baptism was not part of Paul's answer. Baptism is only discussed later (v. 33).

2. Baptism does not wash away your sins.

There are religious groups that believe baptism washes away sins, but carefully looking at the whole context of salvation in Scripture will show us otherwise. According to 1 John 1:7, one thing is able to wash away all our sins. What is it?

_____

_____

_____

Remember, you are cleansed from your sins the moment you personally trust in Jesus Christ as your Savior. You are baptized after that point.

This truth is extremely important. If baptism were able to wash away sin, then Jesus' death would be unnecessary. You are cleansed with the shed blood of Christ, not with water (Hebrews 9:11–14; Revelation 7:14).

3. Baptism does not earn you special favor with God.

Some churches teach that baptism is a means of earning grace. However, grace is by definition *undeserved*. You cannot earn something that is given freely (Ephesians 2:8–9)! In that sense, there is no such thing as grace earned by works. You cannot earn gifts—especially God's gifts! It is an instrument in God's gracious plan for your growth, it is a means by which God grows you.

▶ Part 2: Communion

The second ordinance of the church is communion, the Lord's Table, the Lord's Supper, or the "breaking of bread" (Acts 2:42). These terms are used interchangeably. Communion refers to a corporate celebration of the Lord's victorious sacrifice on our behalf. In this ordinance, the body of believers drinks together from the fruit of the vine (representing Christ's blood) and eats bread (representing Christ's body) together. The object is not so much shared nourishment as it is a visual proclamation of our Lord's death and our union with him. As with baptism, there is confusion about this practice. Therefore, let us study what the Bible has to say about it.

The Purpose of Communion

Like believer's baptism, communion was commanded by the Lord and is a memorial of his sacrificial death on the cross. Luke 22:17–20 records the very first observance of the Lord's Table. Christ had entered Jerusalem with his disciples just prior to his crucifixion. He had them prepare the Passover meal, a memorial meal that was celebrated annually by Jews. The Passover was a God-ordained celebration which commemorated the Jews' deliverance from Egypt by the Lord. Just before the Exodus from Egypt (some fifteen centuries before Christ's earthly ministry), each Jewish family had been commanded to sacrifice a lamb so that God's wrath against Egypt would pass over them (Exodus 12:13).

Almost 1500 years later, Christ entered Jerusalem and died during the Passover celebration. The symbolism here is rich: Christ is the new Passover Lamb, slain to provide salvation from God's wrath against sin for all who believe (1 Corinthians 5:7)! The Old Testament sacrifices were a foreshadowing of Christ's sacrificial death (Colossians 2:17, Hebrews 10:1). At the institution of the Lord's Table, Christ identifies himself as the perfect and final Passover Lamb, his death providing deliverance from sin.

What is Christ called in John 1:29?

What does John say Christ will do?

_____

_____

_____

Compare Hebrews 10:4 with 1 John 1:7. What does Christ do that Old Testament sacrifices could not do?

_____

_____

_____

Unleavened Bread

The bread which Christ used in the Lord's Supper was the unleavened bread of the Passover celebration. Leavening (yeast) is often used in Scripture as a symbol for sin. Christ was sinless—a lamb without blemish or spot (1 Peter 1:19). Unleavened bread symbolizes this sinless innocence of our Lamb.

Read Luke 22:7–20, and answer the following questions:

- In verse 19, what did Christ use to represent his body?

_____

_____

_____

- When would Christ's body be "broken" (v. 19; see v. 15)?

_____

_____

_____

- Jesus instructed the disciples to eat the bread "in remembrance of me" (v. 19). What does that mean?

_____

_____

_____

- Following the bread, Christ used something as a representative of his blood (v. 20). What was it?

_____

_____

_____

- Why was Christ's blood so important for our salvation? (See Hebrews 9:22 and 1 John 1:7.)

_____

_____

_____

The apostle Paul used that first observance of communion to teach later believers how and why to continue it. Read 1 Corinthians 11:23–31. Christ said that the cup and the bread were to be taken "in remembrance of me" (v. 25). Paul concludes in verse 26 that when we eat the bread and drink from the cup we "show the Lord's death." The bread and juice are symbols which help us remember and show Christ's death!

Communion is first of all a remembrance that memorializes Christ's death. However, it is also a reminder of something else (1 Corinthians 11:26 and Luke 22:16 & 18). What is it?

_____

_____

_____

No wonder the Lord's Supper is so precious to Christians! It is a memorial of Christ's death for our sins and a reminder that Christ will return to take us to be with him in heaven! There is indeed cause for a memorial celebration. Yet, it must also be observed solemnly and carefully.

Participating in Communion

In 1 Corinthians 11:27–31, Paul warns against taking the Lord's table "unworthily," or in an unworthy manner. The Lord is serious about this warning—what are some extreme examples of consequences for those who abused the Lord's Supper (v. 30)?

_____

_____

_____

Because of Paul's warning, we need to be careful to honor the Lord as we remember his death:

1. *Only Christians should partake of the Lord's Supper.*

   Anyone who has not trusted Jesus Christ as Savior cannot "discern the Lord's body" (take communion with understanding and judgment, v. 29). Even the word *communion* itself reminds us that all who partake together in the bread should be one body in Christ. As Paul says, "The bread that we break, is it not a participation in the body of Christ? Because there is one bread, we who are many are one body, for we all partake of the one bread" (1 Corinthians 10:16b–17). Communion is for Christians!

2. *Only Christians who are growing in fellowship with God should partake of the Lord's Supper.*

Between the warnings in 1 Corinthians 11:27 and 29 is a command in verse 28. What is it?

_____

_____

_____

What promise is given to people who evaluate or "judge themselves" (v. 31)?

_____

_____

_____

In the Lord's Supper we look *backward* to the death of Christ, *inward* to our own hearts, and *forward* to his coming.

Psalm 139:23–24 is a prayer of self-examination that King David wrote and is a good passage to consider during this time of self-examination and confession. Once you are sure that there is no unconfessed sin causing you to avoid praying or having fellowship with the Lord and other believers, you are free to celebrate the Lord's Supper.

3. *Christians partake of the Lord's Supper reverently.*

Communion is not something to be taken lightly. Rather, it is a time of worship, remembering Christ's death. If communion is intended to be a memorial of Christ's death for you, what should your mind dwell on during the communion service (in addition to making sure that you have repented of your sin)? Be specific.

_____

_____

_____

4. Christians partake of the Lord's Supper in unity.

The Lord's Supper provides the church an opportunity to fellowship with the Lord (vertically) and with one another (horizontally). It is not a private ordinance, but a public one, one for which "the disciples came together" (Acts 20:7). Indeed, it seems that the Lord's Supper was commonly (if not exclusively) observed in conjunction with a love feast, a meal taken together as a symbol of the church's family-like unity.

The Lord's supper is "the simple rite which at once expressed the domestic (family) idea of the church and the worth of Christ's death while it separated the partakers from the crooked generation and bound them into one" (Alexander Maclaren, *The Acts of the Apostles*, 24). In other words, celebrating the Lord's supper marks off believers from outsiders, binds those believers together as a family, and portrays the good news of Jesus that unites them—all at the same time!

Sadly, the church at Corinth had been abusing this celebration. It had become a huge feast for the rich, while the poor had nothing, promoting division rather than unity (1 Corinthians 11:18–22 and 33–34). This is the opposite of observing communion in a worthy manner. The church at Jerusalem provides a far better example in Acts 2:42–44. What four things did Christians continue doing (v. 42)?

_____

_____

_____

_____

What was their attitude toward each other (v. 44)?

_____

_____

_____

A final note about communion is in order. Unlike baptism, which is practiced only once following salvation, the Lord's Supper is repeated. Why? (See 1 Corinthians 11:26.)

_____

_____

_____

Communion is one of the ways that the boundaries of the gospel are established. In a sense, the church publicly unites and proclaims, "We all have believed in the death of Christ in our place—we all believe!" Because of this, the church must protect unbelievers or people who have strayed from the Christian faith from participating as though they are right with God. This practice of guarding the Lord's Supper is called "close" communion. People who are accountable and in good fellowship with a biblical local church should feel welcome joining with other biblical assemblies in this wonderful ordinance. Unbaptized believers, rebellious or nominal, and Christians who have strayed from accountability to a local assembly should quickly turn back to Christ and his church so that they can be assured of their salvation and express their confident joy by sharing in the Lord's Supper. Until they show their faith in obedience and unite with a local assembly, this person should refrain from the Lord's Supper.

▶ Scripture Memory

Matthew 28:19–20

Go therefore and make disciples of all the nations, baptizing them in the name of the Father and of the Son and of the Holy Spirit, teaching them to observe all things that I have commanded you; and lo, I am with you always, even to the end of the age.

1 Corinthians 11:26

For as often as you eat this bread and drink this cup, you proclaim the Lord's death till He comes.

▶ Check Your Progress

What are the three most significant things you learned in this lesson? Why are they important?

1. _____

   _____

   _____

2. _____

   _____

   _____

3. _____

   _____

   _____

Answer the following questions to measure your understanding of baptism and the Lord's Supper:

1. What won't baptism accomplish?

   _____

   _____

   _____

2. What are the biblical reasons for being baptized?

   _____

   _____

   _____

3. What is the prerequisite for baptism?

_____

_____

_____

4. Why is infant baptism unbiblical?

_____

_____

_____

5. What is the purpose of communion? What do the bread and juice represent?

_____

_____

_____

6. What is involved in partaking of the Lord's Supper in a worthy manner?

_____

_____

_____

7. What should you be thinking about during the communion service?

_____

_____

_____

Check off the following verses only when you can say them from memory:

☐ Matthew 28:19–20

☐ 1 Corinthians 11:26

▶ **Notes and Questions**

The Word of God

▶ Introduction

To say that the Bible is important is an understatement. Indeed, it is central to every part of Christianity. But why is it important? From where did it come? How can you understand it? How does it apply to you?

The answers to these questions are vital to your continued spiritual growth. You need to learn to understand the Bible and apply it to your everyday life, and there is no better place to learn about it than from the Bible itself. Let's dig in!

▶ Inspiration of Scripture

Second Timothy 3:16 is a key passage on the inspiration of the Bible. The beginning part of the verse teaches that the Bible is inspired. The Greek phrase which has been sometimes translated "inspiration of God" can be understood literally as "God-breathed" or "breathed out by God." The inspiration of the Bible refers to the process by which God "breathed out" the words of Scripture through human instruments—the writers. The result is that the text of the Bible is God's message, not man's message.

Instruments

When a musician plays a trombone, he blows air through it. The trombone affects the sound, making it different from a trumpet or a tuba. Yet, the trombone is not credited with creating the music. The talent and creativity belong to the musician. The music is his. Audiences applaud trombonists, not trombones. They were only instruments which the musician used to accomplish his purpose. God used men to write the Bible. The Bible is much more than the words of men—it is God's Word!

Some people teach that the Bible merely contains the Word of God. Use 2 Timothy 3:16 to discover what is wrong with that statement.

(Note: Some people believe that there is only one English version of the Bible that is inspired. That belief is not grounded in Scripture.)

How could the Bible be God's Word when it was actually written by men? Second Peter 1:20–21 tells us. What does verse 20 teach about the Bible?

_____

_____

_____

The statement that "no prophecy of the Scripture comes from someone's own interpretation" means that Scripture did not originate with men. The writers of Scripture did not write their own (private) opinions; they wrote God's Word. What does verse 21 teach about the Bible?

_____

_____

_____

Scripture writers did not write of their own volition (will). Rather, they were carried along ("moved") by the Holy Spirit. They picked up pens to write, but the words were God's. Acts 27:15 uses the same word for a ship being driven by wind. Just as wind fills a sail and drives a ship, God's Spirit filled and "drove" the writers of Scripture.

Because the Bible is the Word of God, it is without error—a teaching referred to as the inerrancy of Scripture. In John 17:17 Jesus states that God's Word is _____.

It is impossible for God to breathe out falsehood or error. The Bible teaches that Scripture is absolutely reliable. No matter what topic the Bible speaks about, it is accurate. God knows his science, history, and geography, as well as his theology.

What gives us confidence in God's promises in Titus 1:2?

_____

_____

_____

What does Jesus say about the Bible in John 10:35b?

_____

_____

_____

Jesus is even more specific in Matthew 5:18. Read it. The jot (yod) and tittle he referred to are the smallest parts of Hebrew letters. The tittle is the very slight corner which makes two Hebrew letters different. The yod (pronounced "yode") is the smallest letter. Jesus' statement was similar to the modern phrase "dot your 'i's and cross your 't's."

What was his point?

_____

_____

_____

Matthew 5:18 teaches the following two essential aspects of inspiration:

1. The very *words* are Scripture and, therefore, inspired and inerrant. (This is referred to as verbal inspiration.)

2. The *entirety* of the text is Scripture and, therefore, is inspired and inerrant. (This is referred to as plenary inspiration.)

Can I Trust Translations?

Inspiration refers to the Bible, not the authors. The writers were not inspired. The text is inspired. The translations of the text are not inspired either, since the only thing that was inspired was the original, ancient document. However, our translations of today share the authority, accuracy, and power of the originals when they accurately translate the same meaning that God originally intended for the Bible to have. So today when we hold an accurate translation, we hold the very Word of God.

▶ Benefits of Scripture

We learned from 2 Timothy 3:16 that the Bible is inspired. The verse also explains that the Bible is "profitable"—it will successfully accomplish four tasks. What are they?

1. _____ (what is right: belief) This word specifically refers to the Bible as a teacher. Most of all, it teaches us about God's character and God's will.

2. _____ (what is not right: belief) This word refers to a strong rebuke. The Holy Spirit uses the Bible to prick our consciences about our sin. Scripture exposes to us our sinfulness.

3. _____ (how to get right: behavior) This is similar to setting a broken bone or straightening a crooked spine. Scripture gives spiritual mending—it sets us right again.

4. _____ (how to stay right: behavior) This word is similar to child-training. As parent to child, the Bible trains and disciplines us, bringing us to spiritual maturity.

It is obvious that the Bible is helpful, but what specific tasks has God designed the Bible to accomplish?

1. *The Bible is essential for salvation.*

What does 2 Timothy 3:15b say that Scripture is able to do?

_____

_____

_____

Were it not for Scripture, we would not know our lost condition, much less that Jesus died to provide our salvation. How is saving faith developed in non-believers according to Romans 10:17?

_____

_____

_____

Romans 1:16 says that the Bible is "the power of God _____."

2. *The Bible is essential for Christian growth.*

Scripture paints a vivid picture when it says that you are "born again" at the point of salvation. You are a Christian, but you are only a baby Christian. You need to grow!

First Peter 2:2 speaks of spiritual growth. From what do babies get nourished?

What is spiritual milk for the baby Christian? (See also Hebrews 5:13–14)

_____

_____

_____

How often do babies eat?

_____

_____

What would happen to a baby who did not eat?

_____

_____

What does this passage teach regarding your "feeding" on Scripture? How often do you need it? Why? (See Job 23:12, Acts 20:32, and 1 Thessalonians 2:13)

_____

_____

_____

3. *The Bible is essential for godly living.*

The writer of Psalm 119:9 asked a question that every Christian struggles with: how can I be clean from sin? What is his answer at the end of the verse?

_____

_____

_____

Psalm 119:11 is very similar. Explain it in your own words.

_____

_____

_____

Before Jesus ascended into heaven, he prayed for his disciples and all future Christians, as recorded in John 17. One request was that we would be "sanctified"—made holy. How are Christians sanctified according to John 17:17?

_____

_____

Many Christians say they want to grow, yet they never spend time in God's Word. Scripture is clear that fruitful Christians will be those who consistently study and apply God's Word.

4. *The Bible is essential for knowing God personally.*

Remember, the Bible is not merely a book; it is God's word. It is God's self-revelation—what He has chosen to tell us about Himself. In the words of A. W. Tozer, "The Bible is not an end in itself, but a means to bring men to an intimate and satisfying knowledge of God, that they may enter into Him, that they may delight in His Presence, may taste and know the inner sweetness of the very God Himself in the core and center of their hearts." (A. W. Tozer, *The Pursuit of God* [Camp Hill, PA: Christian Publications, 1982], p. 10.)

Think of Scripture as an Autobiography

The main topic of Scripture is a person, not a program. Scripture teaches us about sin and salvation. It addresses relationships with spouses, employers, children, servants, and persecutors. It is filled with both good and bad examples. It tells us what God expects. It brims with promises. Yet, the Bible is first and foremost an autobiography. It is God revealing himself to his people. When you read it, don't just look for commands, promises, and examples. Look for God!

Jesus tells us in John 5:39 that the Scriptures—even the Old Testament, written before his physical birth—"bear witness" of him. The Pharisees diligently studied the Scriptures and missed a crucial point: They failed to see Christ. The Scriptures are intended to bring us into communion with God, they are not given to make experts about God.

▶ Sufficiency of Scripture

For years, Bible-believers have affirmed that "the Bible is our only rule of faith and practice." This means that the Bible is the ultimate authority on what we should believe and how we should live. However, many men and churches teach that the Bible is a good starting place, but must be supplemented by tradition, psychology, and so on.

We looked at 2 Timothy 3:16 in our discussion about inspiration. Verse 17 goes on to say that the Bible will make Christians spiritually mature ("complete") and fully prepared for ministry. Based on the fact that Scripture can do all of those things, what "charge" does Paul give to the young pastor, Timothy, in 2 Timothy 4:1–2?

_____

_____

_____

Sadly, many preachers today seem to preach anything but the Bible. There is a reason for that. 2 Timothy 4:3–4 says that people will eventually refuse to hear the Bible. What will they want instead?

_____

_____

_____

Although the Bible is thought by many to be antiquated or out of touch, Scripture itself teaches that God's Word alone contains everything we need to know about how to live. Christians from the city of Berea were commended for their attitude toward the Bible and Bible teachers. How did they respond to the preaching of God's Word (Acts 17:10–11)?

_____

_____

_____

Pastors are only helpful to the extent that they direct people to Scripture. Indeed, this very booklet is only helpful to the extent that it points you to Scripture. Your faith and convictions must rest securely on Scripture, not hearsay or opinion. The Bible alone is God-breathed and, therefore, is both helpful and sufficient.

▶ Application of Scripture

Now that you know your need for Scripture, let's be very practical: How do you go about Bible study? Joshua 1:8 gives a three-step process.

1. **Read it.**

   "This book of the law shall not depart out of your mouth" (Joshua 1:8a).

   What are some excuses that Christians give for not reading Scripture?

   _____

   _____

   _____

   How would you respond to those excuses from Joshua 1:8?

   _____

   _____

   _____

   Deuteronomy 6:6–9 is a similar passage. According to these verses, when and how often should you speak about and consider God's Word?

   _____

   _____

   _____

   Reading Scripture with understanding is not easy. You need help! First Corinthians 2:14 teaches that the unsaved ("natural") person cannot and will not "accept the things of the Spirit of God" (Scripture). Why not?

_____

_____

_____

"Texts will often refuse to reveal their treasures till you open them with the key of prayer."

—C. H. Spurgeon, *Lectures to My Students*, 42

By contrast, the Christian ("the spiritual person") is able to discern ("judge") Scripture. Why? He, through the Holy Spirit, has illumination (v. 16). As a Christian, you have the Author of Scripture living in you, helping you to understand and apply what it means!

(Note: The ministry whereby the Holy Spirit helps you to understand Scripture is called "illumination." It will be covered in Lesson 9.)

Write out the prayer uttered in Psalm 119:18 and explain it.

_____

_____

_____

_____

_____

_____

2. *Think about it.*

"But you shall meditate on it day and night" (Joshua 1:8b).

Meditation in Scripture is not thoughtlessness. Rather, it is thinking about Scripture with an emphasis on personal application so that it can be obeyed.

Hmmm...

The Hebrew word that is translated as "meditate" in Joshua 1:8 literally means to moan or mutter. It communicates the idea of deep thought, as though someone were muttering to himself under his breath, so consumed in his concentration that he is oblivious to those around him. God commands you to meditate—think about the Word especially regarding its application to your life (Ps 1:1–2; 119:97–99).

Included in meditation is Scripture memory. You cannot always carry a Bible, but you can carry portions of it in your memory. Memorization is the only way the people of God *could* carry the Bible before the printing press made it possible for common individuals to afford and carry a copy of their own. Read Psalm 119:11 again and explain how it addresses Scripture memory.

_____

_____

_____

3. *Obey it.*

"...so that you may be careful to do according to all that is written in it" (Joshua 1:8c).

Here is the most difficult step of the three, yet the most important. Reading the Bible is good, but obeying it must follow directly. You must apply what you read in Scripture to your everyday life! One of the dangers of spending time in God's Word without applying it is that we begin to deceive ourselves. We think that we are godly when we are not!

James 1:22–25 discuss two different kinds of people. Who are they and what is the difference between them?

_____

_____

_____

Obedience to Scripture demands a difficult thing: change. You must be ready to begin doing things the Bible commands and stop doing things the Bible forbids. This process of change has a final goal: that you should become more and more like Jesus Christ (e.g., 2 Corinthians 3:18).

Stuart Custer, a godly Bible teacher and scholar, writes, "What is in the Bible is not there just to give you historical background or theological precision; it's there to make you what you should be and to mold your understanding of Scripture, so that it may mold your character and transform you into the kind of person that God wants you to be."[1]

Joshua 1:8 does not end with a command, but with a promise of God's empowerment for Joshua as he submits to the Scriptures. God's gracious response to his people's faithfulness is the

[1] Stewart Custer, "Biblical Balance" in *Balance*, vol. 20, No. 4, p. 2.

consistent pattern presented in the Bible. If you read, apply, and obey the Bible as you grow in love for the Lord, God promises to respond with grace, as James says, "he will be blessed in his doing" (James 1:25). God's promise of grace and his enabling presence should prompt us to get to work!

▶ Review

- The Bible is inspired—it is God's Word, not man's; it is therefore without error.

- The Bible is sufficient—it is the only guide that we need for faith and practice. It needs no supplements or outside help.

- The Bible is profitable—it faithfully brings about transformation in thinking and behavior.

- The Bible must be personally applied—read it, think about it, and obey it. The goal of Bible study is change into Christ's character.

▶ Scripture Memory

2 Timothy 3:16

All Scripture is breathed out by God and profitable for teaching, for reproof, for correction, and for training in righteousness.

1 Peter 2:2

Like newborn infants, long for the pure spiritual milk, that by it you may grow up into salvation.

Psalm 119:18

Open my eyes, that I may behold wondrous things out of your law.

▶ Check Your Progress

What are the three most significant things you learned in this lesson? Why are they important?

1. _____

_____

_____

2. _____

_____

_____

3. _____

_____

_____

Answer the following questions to measure your understanding of the Word of God:

1. What is meant by the following terms?

   Inspiration

   _____

   _____

   Inerrancy

   _____

   _____

Sufficiency

_____

_____

Illumination

_____

_____

Meditation

_____

_____

Application

_____

_____

2. Explain what is meant by "our rule for faith and practice."

_____

_____

_____

3. What is inspired?

_____

_____

_____

4. What three steps of Bible study are found in Joshua 1:8?

    _____

    _____

    _____

5. What is the goal of your personal Bible study?

    _____

    _____

    _____

6. What can you do to begin to benefit from your own study of God's Word?

    _____

    _____

    _____

Check off the following verses only when you can say them from memory:

☐ 2 Timothy 3:16

☐ 1 Peter 2:2

☐ Psalm 119:18

▶ Notes and Questions

PRAYER

▶ Introduction

Few Christians, if any, would deny the importance of prayer. Andrew Murray refers to prayer as "the very pulse of the spiritual life" (Andrew Murray, *The Prayer Life*). Yet, most Christians have many questions about prayer. Sometimes they allow their fears to keep them from learning how to pray.

Although volumes have been written about prayer, as always, the Bible is the best teacher.

▶ What Is Prayer?

A very simple definition of prayer is communication to God. God speaks to you through his Word and you speak to God through prayer. The New Testament uses several different words to describe prayer. Several different words for prayer are used in 1 Timothy 2:1 and Philippians 4:6. What are they?

_____

_____

_____

Prayer: This is the broadest and most common term. It especially focuses on God as the object of worship. It emphasizes personal devotion and reverence.

Supplication: This is a petition or request made to God. It focuses on God as the believer's source of help.

▶ Why Should I Pray?

Prayer is not an option for the believer; it is mandatory. What specific command is given in 1 Thessalonians 5:17? In what sense should we never stop praying?

_____

_____

_____

Prayer is a tremendous privilege. In prayer you have the ear of the God of eternity. Think of it! You have the glorious honor of speaking to the One who created you and saved you. You don't just have to pray. You get to pray! Sadly, many Christians have the same attitude toward prayer that they do toward spinach: both are good for you, but must be endured, not enjoyed. They are missing out!

> "We grow, we wax mighty, we prevail in private prayer."
>
> —C. H. Spurgeon, *Lectures to My Students*

Read the following verses and list some of the many benefits that are gained from biblical prayer.

Hebrews 4:16

_____

_____

Luke 18:1–8

_____

_____

James 4:8a

_____

_____

James 5:15–16

_____

_____

Philippians 4:6–7 (When you pray about your anxieties, what does God give you?)

_____

_____

What three promises does Jesus give in Matthew 7:7?

1. _____

2. _____

3. _____

God is not unwilling to answer prayer. Rather, he is eager!

Read 2 Chronicles 16:7–10. How is God described in 2 Chronicles 16:9?

_____

_____

_____

▶ How May I Be Allowed to Pray?

In our culture of entitlement, it may not occur to us to ask the question, "How may I be allowed to pray?" But it is, nevertheless, worth asking how it is that sinners like us may be given access to make requests of the omnipotent, holy Creator of the universe.

The Grounds of Prayer

Although God is eager to answer our prayers, we must come to him humbly and in faith. God does not answer prayer because we are worthy of his attention. We have nothing by ourselves that could gain our entrance into God's presence. Therefore, we come on the basis of Christ's person and work. He is God's holy Son, and on the basis of his death on the cross for our sins, we have access to the Father (Romans 5:1–2, Hebrews 10:19).

What instruction did Jesus give regarding prayer in John 14:13–14 and John 16:24?

_____

_____

_____

Many Christians close their prayer by saying, "In Jesus' name, Amen," without having any idea what the statement means. To pray in Jesus' name includes two close concepts.

First, it is to pray *with his authority*. In New Testament times a wealthy man who was away from home for an extended time would appoint a faithful servant as his *steward*. The steward could then carry on business *in the name of* his master (i.e., with his master's authority). When you pray in Jesus' name, you are in essence saying, "Father, I know that I have no right to be heard by you, but I come on the basis of my relationship with your Son, Jesus Christ. Because of what he has done for me, I come to you with his authority and righteousness, in his name."

Second, it is to pray according to the will of God. It would be assumed that the steward who was acting for his master and with his master's authority would also be acting according to the wishes of his master. He would not be acting selfishly or against his master's best interests. It is therefore vital that when you conclude your prayer, "in Jesus' name" that you have prayed with his desires in mind, not solely yours. It takes a lifetime of practice to grow in our ability to pray in Jesus' name.

"For we do not present our pleas before you because of our righteousness, but because of your great mercy" (Daniel 9:18).

Only those who have been redeemed by God through repentance from their sins and believing in Jesus Christ can pray in Jesus' name with confidence. John 9 tells the story of Jesus healing a man who was born blind. What does that man say about the prayers of unsaved men in John 9:31?

_____

_____

_____

First Peter 2:9 teaches that every Christian has been made a priest by Jesus Christ. Because of our salvation, we can go *directly* into the presence of the Father—we don't need to go through a human priest. According to Hebrews 4:14–16, we only need one High Priest to gain entrance to the Father. Who is it?

_____

_____

_____

First Timothy 2:5 calls Jesus the _____ between God the Father and men. The Lord Jesus Christ himself is your representative before the Father—you don't need any other priest. You can talk to God directly!

According to Hebrews 7:25, what is Jesus doing on your behalf at this very moment?

_____

_____

_____

What Is God's Name?

Praying in "Jesus' name" is praying on the basis of his position and authority according to his will. Yet, it is also true that the specific names of God remind us to trust in God through our various trials and needs. These names identify God's character for us:

Elohim—the Creator God (Genesis 1:1)
El-Roi—the God Who Sees Me (Genesis 16:13)
El-Shaddai—God Almighty (Genesis 17:1)
Jehovah-Jireh—the Lord Our Provider (Genesis 22:14)
Jehovah-Rapha—the Lord Our Healer (Exodus 15:26)
Jehovah-Nissi—the Lord Our Banner (of Victory) (Exodus 17:15)
Jehovah-Mekaddishkem—the Lord Who Sanctifies You (Exodus 31:13)
Jehovah-Shalom—the Lord Our Peace (Judges 6:24)
Jehovah-Rohi—the Lord Our Shepherd (Psalm 23:1)
Jehovah Tsidkenu—The Lord Our Righteousness (Jeremiah 23:6)

The Conditions of Prayer

Prayer is based on our relationship with God (King to servant). Read the following verses and list the conditions God places on prayer.

Psalm 66:18

_____

_____

Matthew 5:23–24 and 1 Peter 3:7

_____

_____

1 John 3:21–22

_____

_____

John 15:7

_____

_____

1 John 5:14–15

_____

_____

(Note: God's will is revealed in his Word. Biblical promises and principles should regularly guide our prayers and requests for ourselves and others. We desire that our prayers be more consistent with Scripture as we mature spiritually. For example, you don't need to pray for God to "be with" another believer. Rather, thank God that he has already promised to be present with those that love him, or you could pray that God would comfort the person with an awareness of his grace and power (Matthew 28:20b). Pray biblically!)

Hebrews 11:6

_____

_____

Matthew 21:21–22

_____

_____

What does James 1:6–7 say to those who pray with doubt rather than faith? (Some of the best demonstrations of faith are praises and thanksgivings. See Philippians 4:6–7.)

_____

_____

Luke 11:5–8 (also see Romans 12:12b)

_____

_____

Matthew 18:19–20

_____

_____

▶ For What Should I Pray?

Many people feel uncomfortable praying because they don't know how to pray. If that describes you, you are not alone. What did the disciples ask Jesus in Luke 11:1?

_____

_____

In Luke 11:2–4, Jesus answered their request with a model prayer. This prayer—often called the Lord's Prayer—has been memorized and repeated by countless people. However, it was intended as an example of prayer, not merely a prayer to be quoted. It teaches us about the type of prayer that honors God.

"Our Father in Heaven"

Prayer is based on a relationship with our Father. The Lord's Prayer shows how God's children pray on the basis of their relationship with him as their Father.

How does Jesus describe God's willingness to answer prayer in Matthew 7:9–11?

_____

_____

_____

"May Your Name Be Hallowed (Honored)"

Prayer is first, and before anything else, worship. Prayers throughout Scripture are saturated with thankfulness and gratitude. Requests are secondary to the need to worship. It is not rushing to God with our needs as though God is simply a cosmic Santa Claus, but it is coming before him in reverence (See Nehemiah 1:5–11 and Luke 1:46–55.)

According to Psalm 100:4, how should you enter into the Lord's presence (e.g., "courts" and "gates")?

_____

_____

_____

The book of Psalms is your worship textbook. Want to learn to worship? Study the psalms:

1. His character: "Praise the Lord for who he is..."

   - Psalm 86:5, 10, 15

   - Psalm 103:8

   - Psalm 106:1

2. His blessings: "Praise the Lord for what he has..."

   - Psalm 103:1–5, 10–14

   - Psalm 150:2

Prayer is agreeing with God's will and seeking his desires. It is not the stubborn pursuit of sinful desires or selfish desires (James 4:1–3). In Luke 22:42, Jesus made a request of the Father. With what words did he close his prayer?

_____

_____

Prayer is seeking the advance of God's work and kingdom.

Prayer is motivated for God's glory. What is Jesus' motivation for answering prayer, according to John 14:13?

_____

_____

"Give Us Each Day Our Daily Bread"

Prayer is dependence on God for daily provision. It is asking God to meet your needs, not your own selfish desires.

What promise does Scripture make in Philippians 4:19?

_____

_____

_____

According to James 4:3, what is one reason for unanswered prayer?

_____

_____

_____

Read Matthew 6:33 and explain what the "all these things" includes. (See vv. 25, 31.)

_____

_____

_____

"And Forgive Us Our Sins, for We Also Forgive Everyone in Debt to Us"

Prayer is dependent both upon your confession of sin and your forgiveness of others. It is hypocrisy to ignore our sin or hold grudges against others, but still expect God to forgive us. Because of this, God will not deal graciously to those who are proud and ungracious toward others.

What warning does Jesus give in Matthew 6:15?

_____

_____

_____

"And Do Not Bring Us into Temptation"

Prayer should include requests for increased godliness. It asks not only for forgiveness of past sins, but also for protection from future sins.

What specific prayer did Jesus command in Matthew 26:41 that corresponds to the closing of his model prayer?

_____

_____

_____

Jesus mentioned several specific requests in his model prayer, but the Bible has many, many more. Read the following verses as you consider some specific needs that should be in your prayers.

2 Thessalonians 3:1–2 (Hint: The apostle Paul wrote this passage during a missionary journey. What specific requests should you make to God for missionaries?)

_____

_____

_____

Colossians 4:3–4

_____

_____

Matthew 9:37–38

_____

_____

1 Timothy 2:1–5

_____

_____

Matthew 5:44

_____

_____

Hebrews 13:18

_____

_____

James 1:5

_____

_____

James 5:13

_____

_____

Praying Pitfalls

In Matthew 6:5–8 Jesus warns against two errors of religious hypocrites. The first error is the use of payers as a demonstration of supposed spirituality (v. 5). He teaches that pray is a matter of devotion to God, it is not for public show-off. Two commentators of the 1800s say the following:

"Prayer is preeminently a matter between the soul and God; certainly not to be a means of advertising self's piety" (G. Campbell Morgan, *Discipleship*, 24).

"It is a little short of blasphemy to make devotion an occasion for display" (Spurgeon, *Lectures*, 56).

The second error is the use of "vain repetitions." Christ is here describing repetitive and thoughtless phrases which are said out of mere habit. Sadly, the Lord's prayer has been often used in pointless repetition without any thought. At best, this lack sincerity. At worst this is superstitious. Remember, you are praying—not reciting or performing—and your prayer is being listened to by a loving Father.

P-R-A-Y

Jesus' sample prayer is a model to be followed. It demonstrates that prayer begins with worship and moves to requests. The following may help people to remember the important aspects of prayer.

Praise and thanks, Renewal, Asking, and then Yielding

When and Where Can I Pray?

Scripture teaches that you can—and should—pray anytime, anywhere. Remember, 1 Thessalonians 5:17 commands you to "pray without ceasing." And that "pray-on-the-go" command really is possible, for God knows your secret thoughts (Matthew 6:6). Therefore, you can pray silently.

Although Scripture commands constant prayer, it also encourages you to set aside consistent times devoted specifically to prayer. What do you notice about Jesus' pattern of prayer in Matthew 14:23 and Matthew 26:36–39?

_____

_____

_____

What example do you see in Mark 1:35 and Psalm 5:3?

_____

_____

_____

(Since Jesus, God's perfect Son, made consistent, fervent prayer a priority in his life, how can you do less?)

Prayerlessness is essentially arrogance. It is saying to God, "I have no need of You. I can make it alone." How much better to humbly kneel before the Lord and acknowledge, "Lord, I need You. Without You, I can do nothing!"

Public & Private Prayer

The Bible says much about private prayer—times when you pray alone to God, seeking to talk privately (Matthew 6:6). Yet, it also stresses the necessity of public payer—times when groups of believers gather for joint prayer. Notice the following texts and their record of joint payer among fellow Christians: Matthew 18:18–20; Acts 1:14; 4:24–31; 12:12b.

Often Christians are hesitant about praying in front of others. Yet, the Bible clearly teaches the value of joint prayer. Work at it! Become comfortable through experience and practice. And begin at your church's regular prayer times!

Note: For a better understanding of biblical prayer, spend some of your Bible study time reading and meditating on some of the prayers recorded in Scripture. Here are some exemplary prayers from godly men:

- Ezra 9, especially vv. 6–15

- Nehemiah 9, especially vv. 5b–38.

- Daniel 9:4–19

- Psalm 51

▶ Scripture Memory

John 16:24

"Until now you have asked nothing in my name. Ask, and you will receive, that your joy may be full."

Psalm 66:18–19

"If I had cherished iniquity in my heart, the Lord would not have listened. 19 But truly God has listened; he has attended to the voice of my prayer."

Philippians 4:6–7

"Do not be anxious about anything, but in everything by prayer and supplication with thanksgiving let your requests be made known to God. And the peace of God, which surpasses all understanding, will guard your hearts and your minds in Christ Jesus."

▶ Check Your Progress

What are the three most significant things you learned in this lesson? Why are they important?

1. _____

   _____

   _____

2. _____

   _____

   _____

3. _____

   _____

   _____

Answer the following questions to measure your understanding of prayer:

1. On whom does prayer focus?

2. What three promises does Jesus make in Matthew 7:7?

3. What does it mean to pray "in Jesus' name"?

4. Why is it important to know the specific names of God revealed in the Bible?

5. List several conditions of prayer.

6. What is the main benefit of the Lord's Prayer?

_____

_____

_____

7. How is it abused?

_____

_____

_____

8. What are the main components of prayer?

_____

_____

_____

9. What are the two "prayer pitfalls" of Matthew 6:5–8?

_____

_____

_____

10. Why are both private and public prayer so important?

_____

_____

_____

Check off the following verses only when you can say them from memory:

☐ John 16:24

☐ Psalm 66:18–19

☐ Philippians 4:6–7

▶ **Notes and Questions**

_____

_____

_____

_____

_____

_____

_____

_____

_____

_____

_____

_____

_____

_____

_____

_____

Made in the USA
Middletown, DE
24 September 2023

39250611R00077